Between the Lines
Karen O'Connor

♫ DOGHOUSE

Between the Lines

is published by
DOGHOUSE
P.O. Box 312
Tralee G.P.O.
Co. Kerry
Ireland

TEL: +353 (0)66 7137547
www.doghousebooks.ie
email: doghouse312@eircom.net

ISBN 978-0-9565280-7-0

Edited for DOGHOUSE by Noel King

Cover photograph: *A Dry Sunday* by Ray Foley
www.ray.ie

The publisher and poet thank Ulster Bank, Blackpool, Cork for
their sponsorship of this collection.

Further copies available at €12, postage free, from the above
address, cheques etc. payable to DOGHOUSE also PAYPAL -
www.paypal.com to doghousepaypal@eircom.net

Doghouse is a non-profit taking company, aiming to publish
the best of literary works by Irish born or Irish resident
writers. Donations are welcome and will be acknowledged on
this page.
For our 2011 publications, many thanks to

KERRY
EDUCATION
SERVICE
Scríbhís Oideachais Chiarraí

Kerry Education Service.

Printed by Tralee Printing Works, Monavalley Industrial Estate, Tralee, Co. Kerry

for
Andrew and Holly
with love

Acknowledgements are due to the editors of the following where some of these poems, or versions of them, have been published:

Poets Meet Painters Anthology, 2010; Prairie Schooner; Real Imaginings – a Kerry Anthology, 2009; Revival; The Sharp Review; The SHOp; Sixty Poems for Haiti Anthology, 2010; The Stinging Fly; The Stony Thursday Book; Ware Poetry Anthology, 2006.

The Sergeant's Wife was Commended for the Ware Poetry Competition, 2006.

If I was your wife was shortlisted for the Fish International Poetry Prize, 2006 and won 2nd prize in the Clogh Poetry Competition in the same year.

St Michael's was shortlisted for the Fish International Poetry Prize, 2007.

Coring Apples was shortlisted for Writers' Week, Listowel, single poem prize, 2010.

The Doll was Commended for the Aesthetica Creative Works Competition, 2010.

Special thanks to all my family, my brothers, sisters, nieces and nephews for being part of my life.

And to Eileen and Seán for my *cúpla focal as Gaeilge*.

Contents

If I was your wife

dinner wouldn't be ready
or even thought of
when you rounded the bend at six.
I'd be in the yard – barefoot
probably naked,
painting nettles and dock leaves
in bright garish blue,
your children unwashed
your house as you left it
your hunger forgotten,
wondering, as you came to a stop
what had occupied your thoughts
since leaving work.

You wouldn't have felt the need
to wash in the red pan
in the cold back kitchen,
scrubbing to your elbows
futilely trying to erase the oil
crease on your palm,
hooshing water onto your face
blowing out loudly
scrubbing down to your breastbone
leaving your neck red mottled with effort.

You wouldn't have sat at the bottom of the oblong table
waiting for your dinner to be placed
or looked between the rows of your children
at your wife, sitting at the opposite end
one word – *Chef*
or she wouldn't have risen without pause
and passed your seat
to retrieve the brown sauce you demanded,
days the dinner wasn't up-to-much.

If I was your wife
I would have answered, *bollocks*
to your, *Chef*
and told you, *get off your arse and get it yourself.*
But we would never have reached the table
we would have eaten from the earth
raw mud-covered spuds and carrots
laughed as the nettles stung our mouths
made love in the tall grass
the children playing tag in the yard
knowing only the freedom of having nothing
but loving it, embracing it.

We wouldn't have slept in separate beds
with quilts and pillows for solace
but lay on the bare ground
comfortable in each other's arms.

And when the tortured razor-lines of life
tore through our story
you would have held me,
frail, embracing every flaw of my being,
squeezing support, never letting go.

If I was your wife.

Death in Fishnet Tights

Only afterwards I realised I'd met her
the brush of her hand along the nape of my neck
the smell of smoke in my nose hair
the tang of sulphur on my tongue.
She was wearing fishnet tights,
with black curling hair to her shoulders
and she had the whitest skin.
She never spoke – being death it was unnecessary
but as the living threaded in and out of my world
she remained, just beyond the wooden frame
often coming as far as the foot of my bed
and then retreating, as if my life was being written
line by line, and she was waiting
her cue from the wings.

The Dare

Bicycles in the backyard
the dare of 'round the ring'
my father leading the charge
out past the laurel tree
his paunch hindering
his attempt to throw his leg over.

My mother, wafer-thin, laughing
her legs crossed – balancing
coughing out instructions
with no intention of following
just the pretence to get him going
and us cheering and clapping
lining the driveway, waiting for the off.

As she led out her bike he was gone
out the back gate without a glance
leaving her 'bent in two'
and us swarming around her
on our own imaginary bikes
our turning point.

We raced and raced and raced
until his return, much, much later
his face flushed and shimmering
his T-shirt stretched to his back
my mother laughing, *what kept you*?
having never left the yard herself
and us children, excited in their revelry
although the subtext was lost on us.

Fourteen Steps
for Andrew

The garden has reclaimed my flower beds.
The grass, centimetre by millimetre
crawling over the red and yellow bricks
sucking them down,
disappeared, as if they never existed.
Then marching on
to smother the sweet pea stems
strangling the verbena
the sturdy oxalis choking out
its last delicate bud
before succumbing to the approaching force
leaving only the memory of its colour
brightening that western corner
a slight rise that hints at cultivation
a shade variance in the grass
as if sweeter, more delicate here
where moss peat and potash enrich the soil.
For me it signifies my retreat
my failed steps over the uneven ground
my unwillingness to seek help
to allow another's hand to shape my landscape.
And yet you have struggled beneath my weight
brought me out centimetre by millimetre
across the path, the rotting flower baskets,
the uneven steps
to perch me here, in this south-facing niche
surveying nature's triumphs, her adaptability
leaving me to germinate
slowly drawing my head up
tilting to catch the sun
opening my display.

The Wardrobe

That narrow wood door
with its mirror
like a pane of glass.
Inside, one rail, jammed
full of clothes
we'd never seen her wear,
the Bolero fox-fur she'd worn
to someone or other's wedding
back before we were born,
the dresses and Edam cheese
coat with the button-down lapel.
She'd take them out
smooth the pressed wrinkles
someday, she'd say,
I'll go somewhere posh
enough to wear these.
And butterflies would emerge
nested from our last exploration
brightening the room,
she'd throw her head back
and laugh – even the butterflies
found it funny.
Then she'd tie the fox-fur
round my shoulders
slip her Cinderella heels on my feet
and present me to the mirror.
Beyond, the handsome prince
his white horse patient in his waiting
pushing me towards him
her smile in reflection
nodding her assurance
the butterflies sitting in her hair.

Being your mother

I eat the things you spit out
I bend to your will
at night when I hold you
my shoulders breaking
from the strain
of your two-year
two-stone body
like my ribs will crack
and turn to dust
deep inside a place
I never knew existed
I sing, my breath catching
in my throat
your fingers instinctively
milking mine
settling into sleep
and still I hold you
pull you close
my muscles burn
the night ploughs on
but you and I are still suspended
in my mother's arms
her fingers curling in my hair
her breath, like mine
breathing in with yours
so close, I often think
it's you are holding both of us.

The Shape of her History

Like discarded rags
her memory regurgitates
moments, crumpled and bent
often joining unrelated bits
substituting her, for her sisters
strangers, news stories, fiction
until she reassembles
like a collage of many jigsaws
often missing an eye, a cheekbone
a breast. Ill-fitting pieces
raised in relief.
In this state of disassembly
she listens to her parts
slip in and out of joining
trying to fit into
the smooth picture
of her placing.
She is Picasso's
Woman in a Red Hat
in a Turner landscape
her lines – all out of tune
and when she speaks
her language is unrecognisable
like birdsong or baby talk
and deep inside she feels a pain
she has no right to possess
burning between her womb
and her oesophagus
a remnant of truth.

No-Man's-Land

Between them was no-man's-land
the purple landscape creased and wrinkled
vast as the universe.
Words lost in the absent echo
claimed their prize
of narrow lands on the edge
of their respective abyss.
In between, the fertile plain
where she was conceived
worth fighting for
night after night
flares burst on the headboard
illuminating the blood-red trenches
coils of razor wire
strung out along mortar-pitted hills
ragged chunks of flesh and hair
hung as reminders of unsuccessful forays
into the mine-filled middle.
That which neither could surrender
now a wasteland of ice and snow
leaving puckered backs exposed
aching limbs hanging on
to crippling postures
for fear of rolling in
of capitulating.

Drop-off Point

I sat out today
listening to the lambs lament the cut grass
of the football field,
the noise of the German tourists'
wheeled luggage sparked a memory
of that go-cart we made
with the small ball bearing wheels.
A death trap, my mother said
but we could only see perfection
the mobile front axle
giving excellent cornering,
my long legs folded on the plywood body
and your short stubby run to get us going
jumping on behind, screaming from the off
down Mill Lane to the jump-off point
before the road.
How many hundreds of turns
did it take before that one 'bockety' wheel
failed to stop, coming a cropper
with a 1989 John Deere?
That last summer we picked up
the dismembered pieces, lugged
them home, with plans of remodelling
a new improved chassis
a twin exhaust system.
You were gone when I went to call you out.
Unexpected, she said
gone back to live with your parents.
I stood there on the high step
turning away from your grandmother
looking down the long field
to the abattoir, the stink of
blood in my nostrils
a butterfly in my throat
our new exhaust
burning the tips of my fingers.

Waking

He slept at the home place
surprised by the familiar
sound of lambs calling
the crunch of traffic
his father's sighs
stretching the shadows
of a room unchanged.

Each time he woke
he thought he heard her
sing low in the kitchen
accompanied by the radio
the clink of washing glasses
the stir of the fire
her housecoat rustling the stairs
as she came to call him for school
his breakfast waiting on the table
his father out on the mountain
reading the heather, talking to the wind.

He drifted in and out
listening to the murmur of conversation
the susurrus of prayer
the whisper of tears
and knew they were there, together
holding hands over the faded quilt
making arrangements for tomorrow
stretching the night
until the final hour.

Between the lines

another poet draws water
in galvanised buckets
up the narrow passage to Dineen's.
He doesn't have a piggery
or rats the size of cats
but my memory reads between his lines
changing the water to frothy milk
sloshing in the gallon's brimming heat
the fear of spilling the precious cargo
weighed with the overwhelming fear
of meeting one of the giants – slowed by poisoning –
crossing the lane, its beaded eyes staring
down the funnel of our escape.
Knowing the sting of the sally
for every wave that crests the lip
and flows down the side
bread-crumbing our retreat
we stand immobile
moving only the gallons – hand to hand –
pulling against the weight
to relieve the welt of red
rising on our sweating palms.
Our fears growing with the fading light
we settle on skirting – one either side –
shooing and stamping.
He watches us draw level
then ups his bulk on tiny wasted legs
my gallon slipping to my fingertips and gone
my feet gathering speed
until we're home, crying
with the loud tread of his following
and the knowing of what lies ahead.

The birds

are feasting on our bird feeder
the one we filled with peanuts
the day I bought the butterfly wellies
to navigate the swamp of the back garden.
You tried to ease your tongue around the word
butterfly, annoyed when I didn't realise
you wanted to press your cheek to mine
flutter your long lashes
in the kiss your daddy taught you.
I wanted us to go out, air us
blow away the web of self-doubt
that had taken purchase in me.
And we did make the squelching journey
to retrieve the empty feeder
swaying pointedly in the breeze.
You helped me prop its wire cage
against a flowerpot
coaxing nuts along its narrow neck
squealing with delight
as the robins and finches
dipped above our heads
approving of our industry.
Satisfied we had retrieved every stray nut
scurrying along the footpath
we squelched back to hang up our bounty
letting go of your hand for that split second
to hook the feeder in place
I turned to find you joyfully sitting
splashing your hands in the grass
and laughing at the eager birds
diving for cover in the nearby honeysuckle.

Blue Ceramic

Picasso died today, April 8th.
In 1973 I wasn't even aware
of my own self
not to mind the majesty of painters.
Later I saw a plate he made in the flesh
my hand trembled as I
reached across the years
to caress his ceramic half moons
feel the rush of torment
fire up through my fingertips
vibrating my teeth
that pain to create
like needles under the skin.
Often I remember that day
Andrew and his father
standing in the parkland
posing with the house
and inside that strange shaped
blue ceramic
his epithelials scraped on clay
his power glazed over.
I could feel it, even then
metres from the house, pulsing
like the firing had never cooled
and it had burned through
the casing, the floor, the earth
the heat – radiating up
through the soles of my shoes.

My brother rings

the bitch is sick again
she's always got some arse or an elbow
and he's had enough
this is her last chance
if she doesn't cop-on this time
she'll be swimming to Youghal
or starring on the X Factor
singing for her supper.
He talks about hocks, vet bills and cat flu
before moving on to ferreting in Pike's field
laughing at the hard ground of hills and hillocks
neighbours known worldwide in the locality.

He pissed on me when we were children
out by the gable end of the house
always in the shadows.
I stood still – let him piss on me
I harboured physical hatred for that
grown from my mother's love for him
her unflinching belief that he would be 'there for me'
I would spit with temper
not if I was dying would I ask him.

He moves on to Father Jo
he has scour and needs to be segregated
he's worried about dehydration, rehydration
worried the pups will get it.

She was right all those years ago
he is 'there for me'
not the man I thought he was at all.
Still the double of my father
gruff, uncooperative exterior
but soft as Laughing Cow cheese inside
which is how I feel at the moment
mad as a brush, soothed by dog talk and incidentals.

He moves on to fishing
claiming his spot and ending up on his arse in the river
his rival doubled on the bank in stitches
his struggle with full waders makes me laugh
his ability to humiliate himself, endearing.
He might be back on Sunday with the girls
might take Razor and Trixi for a trial on Tuesday night
might need my help.
Now he has to go, can't stay gossiping all night
there's a card game to go to.

Growing Up

Today you walked in my shoes
clip-clopping around the kitchen
beaming at your grown-up self
swaying in impossible heels
eyelashes fluttering
vaseline glistening lips
your miniskirt barely covering
the top of your multicoloured tights
your hips zigzagging
to the stereo's 'gettin jiggy with it'.

I'm not ready to see these small
increments of independence
budding in you. Desperately holding on
to your tiny hand, fleshing out in mine
your reach growing daily
your voice strong and reasoned
sounding out your growing vocabulary.
Between your abundance of smiles
is a hint of defiance
a growing need to assert yourself
to the woman you will become.

In these small glimpses
I'm reminded that I'm the one
with a lot of hard growing to do.

The Orchard

She grows a womb on her pomegranate tree
shrivelled from the scorching temperatures
and arid landscape, the earth grown cavernous
parched from months of nothing
not even a whisper of water.
Under the tree the cat looks up at her dried
leathery prune of a womb, waiting for it to drop.
He'd spent weeks since she first grafted it
caterwauling at the sky, begging it to fall
that fetid meat odour driving his taste buds wild.
But time has grown patience and now he waits
like a true male, for his turn to come
as she does, watching from the shade of the lemon tree
she knows nature has a way of sorting these things
the rain and the duplicity of humans
these are just markers
made to wash away in one turn of tide
leaving the trees fortified with fruit
and her dried womb, swollen
dripping from the old tom's whiskers.

Susurrus

She'd come to say goodbye to the people on the hill
planted to look down on the harbour
warmed by the sun – always watchful.
She paused at the slipway, attracted to the silence
even the water running up the rippled concrete
retreated without a sound, respectful of the dead
pulling her down, the way it ballooned upwards
and ran away at the sides
leaving the surface shimmering.
An English woman with a collie named Jessie
played catch on the fistful of sand
their din pushing her back from the edge
back to the people who took the horizon
the clouds sitting on their shoulders.
She found herself wishing to be here
not tended and visited but abandoned to the elements
the sea roaring up from the dark night
the rain pouring valleys, gushing to the sea
and days like this – a soft sky with a whisper of wind.
She climbed between the headstones
slowly feeling her breath labour under the pull
and sat amongst them
conscious of the hiss of traffic winding the coast road
the whoosh of a silent gull
the soft roar of jets pushing through clouds
and a low hum, almost lost in the ambient sound
like thoughts rising
a fine mist of words
prayers for the living.

Knowing Death

We sit listening to a woman talk
about her good friend, suicide.
Shaking her eighties-styled bangs
she laughs at her decision
then cries because it's all too much.
We sit closer than our skin
listening to her matter-of-fact
life and death, no reasons, no explanations.
That's how you felt, you say
when I died, when they took you
to that empty room
gave you stats, sodium levels, blood pressure.
I talk about the walls that became windows
the characters that appeared and danced
with sweeping scores.
It brings us even closer.
We cry because she killed herself
saved by the sight of new buds on naked branches.
Afterwards I feel warm
your skin snuggled around me
your breath in my mouth.

Hide-and-Seek

We play hide-and-seek.
I squat, the sally branches
my flexible fortress.

I'm forty and the sallies
have grown strong and thick
imprisoned by their bulk.

I'm forty-two and their trunks
wobble before me
barks seeping lemon curd.

I squeeze my child fingers
through their emaciated frame
and lick the juice – lime flavoured.

Then ever so carefully, I draw
their curtain wide and see you
frantically searching for me.

I smile – a child's innocence
your assumption
I always hide in the long grass.

Not this time, I know better
I lifted the grass to hide my snail trail
and wait here.

With no breadcrumbs to follow
you feel the panic rise
calling, calling my name.

I drop my protective curtain
swaying gently back into place
and wait.

You know the rules
you taught me well
I will never tell.

Peace Offering

Tomorrow I'll wait in the breeze
– north, north-east –
bringing an arctic freshness to your perch
carrying my talisman
the eraser for my failings
a new beginning, a child is born
and though I'll travel without
the counsel of wise men, mother
confounded by Jehovah's words
I'll find my way
stand at the sea's gaping mouth
look into its jaws
and tender my votive offering
swaddled in a Santa suit
bald as the day she was born
sporting her Christmas wish of two front teeth
and as flecks of sand crystallise on her long lashes
I'll wait your hand – a whisper, a footprint
'to die is to sleep without dreams'
thirteen years of waiting will be over
tomorrow, Christmas day.

Settling

I lie
feeling my sediment dip
to my shoulder blades
the back of my head
my buttocks and heels
settling slowly beside you
as if my skin was glass
I picture the movement
like a good Guinness
flowing backwards
until I have a creamy head
in my nose, nipples and toes
then, and only then
will you tip me sideways
and drink.

The Interview

Where do you see yourself in three years time?
What strengths would you bring to the job?
These were all questions she had prepared
but when they asked her to list three words
her mother would use to describe her:
bollocks, unreliable, selfish,
bollocks, delusional, useless,
bollocks, druggy, whore
were not going to help her get this job
convince these people to give her a shot
I'm sorry, I don't know, I've just gone ... blank
am .... am ....
myself and my mother have good fun
so I suppose she'd say fun
she could feel her toes curl in her high-heeled shoes
and she'd definitely say I was honest
yah, definitely honest
her toes were curling and she thought she could
feel the tip of her nose stretching, aching forward
and trustworthy, yah trustworthy.
She knew then that the interview was over
not from the interviewer's stifled yawn
or the preceding eye roll
not from the long pause, or the fact that she
kept bringing her hand up to touch the tip of her nose
but from the realisation that she was crying
salt tears streaking her mascara.

The Doll

Like all the hand-me-downs I had presumed her empty
spent, like the elastic of the knitted tights
my weak kidneys forced me to wear
or the shoes whose tongues had tired of talking
lolling to the sides
like dead badgers on my narrow pins
raided by my sisters, cousins in America,
friends of friends-of-ours
who didn't need them anymore.

Her parcel arrived, holding the worst selection of rags
my mother had ever seen
more holed than my rough wear.
Shaking her weary head
she swept the bedraggled bundle into her arms
and squeezed her out from that cloth womb
onto our kitchen floor
her roly-poly body rocking hypnotically to a slow stop
gazing intently at me.

But it was only my insatiable curiosity
that forced me to retrieve her
test her for that wished for chocolate
beneath her painted-on clothes
and keeping her –
to spite my older sisters' pick of parcels.
She was my secret – Matryoshka
from that aged body, dried out, chipped and battered
a baby, pristine, perfect, pure.

St. Michael's

The crucifixion in the boys' school astonished
everyone. By word of mouth a small crowd
gathered. The few dignitaries who were present,
myself included, were thrilled to be asked – had
spent the day in preparation, after all – what is
the etiquette? I decided on purple, it reminds me
of Easter and matched it, by sheer fluke, with a
wide brimmed hat sporting a crown of thorns
– fabulous! The day was surprisingly warm for
April and gave the experience a carnival quality.
I was slightly annoyed by Pontius Pilate who
wore long flowing robes with a gold trim
shimmering in the sun, taking away a little I fear
from my own ensemble. But not to be outdone,
I spat further than anyone, hitting Jesus square
on the cheek as He passed, with such force that He
turned His head and looked at me. I felt
triumphant, having made the prophet change
His view. He dragged on and the small band of
people followed, feeling the excitement of the
event, thinking this might be one of those
moments we look back on and remember. In the
hallway, where they had prepared the pebble-
dashed wall, they mounted the cross and took
time to drive each nail. I had a quick chat with
Judas, who hadn't intended on coming but felt,
somehow, responsible for the whole thing and
therefore couldn't miss it. I was surprised he
hadn't made a better effort with his appearance,
his clothes were old and tattered and smelled of
ages. I wondered why Lazarus hadn't decided to
shut his 'Never Give Up' shop for one afternoon
and come along. Still, perhaps he had only heard
the news at the last minute and couldn't close,
these things happen. As the only woman present,

apart from Her that is, I felt rather honoured. She
of course was dressed in her customary blue,
which didn't really do anything for her – except
make her look washed out. She could at least have
thrown on a smidge of lipstick. I know crucifixions
are a gruesome affair but to be here and in purple,
looking so well, was quite a coup for me. I found
the wait long though, my Marco Tozzi shoes were
definitely built for beauty not for comfort and the
speeches, and there are always speeches, seemed
to drag on a bit. Afterwards they had tea and
sandwiches in the hall and people had the
opportunity to mingle. Judas left early, said he'd
lost his appetite but Pilate hung on. Once I'd come
to terms with his compulsion to repeatedly wash
his hands, he turned out to be extraordinarily
good company. It beat talking to the rest of the
apostles, who'd arrived late then hung around
with long faces; they were always the same, the
dry balls at every party. I left just as Mary
Magdalene arrived. After all I had read The Da
Vinci Code too and I really wasn't able for all
that controversy and debate, when anyone would
know from looking at her, that there wasn't a drop
of royal blood in her veins.

Scales

The rains came as promised
hammering from a brooding sky
swelling the river, rising the sea
and when I looked again
you were there –
flotsam on my front lawn
washed out of the clouds –
a beached whale
your eyes staring in at me
your mouth slack, defeated
wheezing in those last few breaths.
Pushing me back to that store-cupboard room
watching your body heave
your chest rising.
Those vast breaths so deceiving
in and out now on my front lawn
shocked neighbours rush for buckets
to keep you hydrated
calling the marine authorities
who will surely laugh to hear
a whale landed four kilometres from the sea.
And still they struggle to save you
comfort those huge salt tears
while I just watch – useless
even now, the second time around.

The Chair

It was no coincidence your window faced east
the light poking through the dense laurel
stepping across the lane, through that strip
of waste ground, onto Regan's front lawn.
The first thing I'd see when I rounded the bend
the only glimmer, in the complete darkness of country
the walk from the train, those nights you couldn't
persuade him to shift himself and collect me.
And I'd know you'd be there
a novel resting on your knees
your hands wringing out each minute
unable to relax, until you heard the back door
my struggle up the stairs. You'd beam at me
throw out your arms, hug and kiss me
pull up the chair, you'd say.
And I'd sit there until it was time to go to bed
talking about my week, about trying to find my feet.
His shout from the kitchen,
nobody ran away with you then?
was left unanswered, as we trawled through our days
for the struggles, the laughs, the mundane
just to sit there an extra ten minutes.
Some nights we'd watch The Late Late
to see what fancy had ignited his interest
his comments to the television
sending us into smothered laughter
or I'd sneak downstairs
when we were sure he was glued to the box
and make ham sandwiches
with mustard and black pepper
laughing like schoolgirls at the thought of him –
have I no mouth on me?
That chair was hard and unyielding
your bras always stretched across its back
piled with clothes and books, it was where you sat
to comb your hair, add a hint of lipstick:
the best seat in the house.

Coring Apples

i.m. Tom Mulqueen

I remember my father's weathered hands
like parched earth, the way the chemo
grew out of his nails
the way his hair grew back
white as frost and curling
like my baby daughter's.
I remember he never got to meet her
never knew it was a girl
but that was right, he'd said
that he would go – to make room.
I remember trying not to notice
the hospice beds emptying around him
the tremble in his hand
as he brought the beaker to his lips
the way his eyes wandered
to the window and the tower beyond.
I remember sitting by my father's bed
painstakingly peeling apples
a ribbon of skin furling on my lap
a sign, he'd said, of a steady hand –
safe hands to leave things in.
I remember his palms pressed with earth
from planting winter saplings
or rhythmically folding, creasing, folding
while reciting from memory
verse after verse of Clifford or Kipling.
I remember my father's weathered hands
fingers laced around the worn beads
of his Medjugorje rosary
wax-warm and motionless
the skin brown like apple cores
and thin as tissue paper
and I remember thinking
how they were – strong, safe hands.

Grain

On the wood of the bathroom floor
there's a profile of an eagle
his one eye visible
big and round – pitch pupil
with a pin of white
his feathers full
watching the branches sway
gravity pressure pumping
the smell of the clouds.
I press my face to his
smell the dust between the floorboards
feel his spirit press my cheek
his tears wet
as he takes the strain
pushing, pushing, rising up
away from the unending search for food
away from the syringe
the smell of sweat
the wetness between my legs
and that awful moaning in my head
up, up to where the clouds sit far below
the blue swallows us – blinding
before I finally close my eyes
and walk out the only door available
closing it quietly behind me.

Holly

I find pieces of you
in my hair, my clothes
thorny parts in my womb
berry-red and seeded there
gloss-green pieces on my skin
under my fingernails
between my toes.
Remnants in my childhood
– those woven branches
of frost-softened drupes
and spine-tipped evergreens –
my runaway fortress
from hormones and adolescence
seasons decorating the house
with fresh-cut berry branches
hung beneath the Sacred Heart lamp
watching it grow old with the year
browned with the heat of the fire
its leaves curling inwards
their lustre fading
flaking into March
like flecks of dried blood
falling to the 'purtie' shelf below.
Now it opens the season on each day
sparks a match in the darkness of winter
holds a smile in its saying.

He stole my soul

with a Fuji instamatic
capturing my essence
stretch marks, slipped to broken veins
wobbles and sags
snapped, like knicker elastic
crossing my shaved legs
in my favourite Basic Instinct pose.
He deserted
a knowing smile pinned
leaving me vacant
hollowed out from the inside
separated from other beings
who moved in positive directions.
I remained the negative
repelling all advances
drowning in circles of him
in colours of that day
as autumn slipped from trees
reflecting his eyes, his lips
like a thief gliding between the crowds
his pocket bulging with my soul
never looking back
at the empty seat he left behind.

Sacred Bamboo

Watering the sacred bamboo
swirl of dirt water
reminds me of the mud pies
we used to make as children
watching them bake in the sun
finely crafted into cakes
evenly spaced on the bonnet
of the old Ford Anglia.

Or the sloe wine we toiled for hours on
produced by the bottle
buried in the acre to ferment,
we could never agree the exact location
when the exhumation date was due.

Now we share baking tips
swapping recipes, comparing tastes.
Why can't I mention my broken heart
or the effort it takes to speak of insignificant things?
Why can't you hold me
tell me everything will be okay
this too will pass?

Could it be the remnants of those stories
you conjured out of tiredness
to ensure our hush – terrified,
driven by our mortal fear of the Glebe
those overhanging branches and dense air,
the grey walls of Doody's
draped with the skeletons of vines,
and the black door where your stories
hung his wife each Sunday?

I look at this scrawny scrap of a thing
no more sacred than the pot it sits in
and know you tried to tell me
in your own way
it wasn't worth the money
or my love, but all I could see
was the need in it
a thing that you could never see.

The Good Son

The wall stood at two-foot-two
the treble had no room for manoeuvre
the water jump – just before the oxer –
left you completely off your stride.
The wall was the decider
the one everyone feared.
I was first to go, Raimondo D'Inzeo, riding Bellevue.
I did a slow circuit
to make sure of the sequence and my approach
and then I applied my heels.
Belle led into the first beautifully
he was right on every turn, every landing
until the water – pulling his head up
at the blue pan – forcing me to
take a shorter approach to the wall
rising up, kicking out in mid air
rattling the top post but it held over the last
a time of one minute, three seconds.
My sister was next, Eddie Macken, riding Boomerang.
She approached the first way too quickly
wasn't making the four-hoof clopping sound
and I made her go back and start again
told her next time she'd be disqualified.
She had a passable round
rattling the brush on the third
and insisting on cleaning her shoe of dog shit
before finally attempting the wall.
I could see it straight away, her approach was all wrong
she stood way off – the angle too steep –
to be fair, she only clipped the top bar
but it was already loose from my round
and it came crashing down –
four faults in a time of three minutes.
My older brother was last to ride
he was Harvey Smith riding Bulldozer.
No matter what rider he was, he always rode Bulldozer
but he never seemed to notice.
He had no approach at all, no rhythm in his limbs.

He nearly died when he was a baby
or so our mother kept telling us.
Some days I wished he had.
She always took his side, even when he was wrong.
He managed to spill the blue pan –
almost impossible even if you tried –
and refused the wall twice
said it wasn't fair, it was too high.
Norma was happy with second.
She helped me to make a podium out of milk crates.
Raimondo D'Inzeo on two crates – the winner
Norma next on one crate
and James just standing on the ground.
But he arrived with Mammy in tow
said I cheated, that he should have won
and mother agreed, asking me to step down
and let him take his rightful place.
I was in full victory salute
my arms stretched above my head
I just stepped off – kicking out as I did
sending the crates screeching into the oxer.
My mother called *bad loser* to my retreating back
my cheeks burning with indignation
and him, the tool, wrecking the jump
to take the crates and claim a prize he didn't deserve.
Years later he got TB
probably in his system all that time, my mother said,
when I could have made him feel special but didn't.
I remember the time I stabbed him
through the foot with a pitchfork
if anyone truly deserved it – he did
the good son.

Your Place

There's talk of cutting down your trees
the ones that reached across to touch your window
those long skeletal fingers exfoliating the house
back to your favoured blue
as if they too realised your absence
the cast of darkness left
the dampness rising through the roof.
How much those walls miss you – they're weeping still.
How unrecognisable it is as your place
the kitchen table so much smaller
without our feet shuffling underneath
the delft press overhead – its doors ajar
your papers always stacked
behind that last slatted plate
but it's more than just your things
or lack of them – it's light
how small the windows seem, how dark.

Instruments of Leisure
for Tom & Bridie

Sweeping the yard
he pauses to watch the late afternoon sun
pierce the peak of the palm trees.
He swings the brush
a long, slow, sweeping movement
cascading midges in his wake
extending into full swing position
his arms crook his neck
and he looks out at the invisible ball
arcing through the evening sky
a good strike – sweet
heading for the clouds.
He adjusts his stance
stepping lightly from foot to foot
and swings again
piling through, his feet planted
his hips fluid to their finishing position.
Just as he tees up the third
her knuckles rap the glass
three short, sharp, taps.
Smiling, he bows to the shadow,
lifts his cap to the spectators
acknowledging their applause,
and pushes the brush before him
jauntily swaying to the sound of evening.

God on the Landing

The turkey is roasting
his ass golden in the oven
the smell of flowery Golden Wonders
makes my taste buds tingle
heightened by the sprouts earthy fragrance
slipping beneath the kitchen door
and walking up the stairs before me
giving a sharp charge to the air
pockets of Coty L'Aimant
linger in your wake
whisper of your slippers
your cardigan's brush
with covered walls
bringing music –
bells and trumpets
proclaiming the
impending meal
the division of presents
the annual game of 110.
I wait at your door
my hand poised to knock
halfway between inhale and exhale
I realise it's your birthday –
2009 years my saviour.
I'm left shattered
fragmented into tiny shards
raining to the landing
I only just realised
God doesn't live here anymore.

Dúirt Sí Liom

Love is for people who can't dance.
Memory chooses what it likes
with no regard for the truth.
Grammar is like sword swallowing
you'll know when you get it wrong.
Snuff never killed anyone.
Tabhair dom do lámh, she'd say
holding up my palm
to the cast from the kitchen window
she'd narrow her eyes
look deep into the furrows
I lost my Gaeilge between my hand and my head
the life of a language is to speak it
touching her right fist to her left breast
remember, she'd whisper, *na rudaí beaga*
and she'd run her index finger
along my lifeline
as if she could iron it, straighten it out
coax its shadow to lengthen.

* Dúirt Sí Liom: She said to me
* Tabhair dom do lámh: Give me your hand
* Gaeilge: Irish
* na rudaí beaga: the little things

Inside Out

You show me your belly
and demand to see mine
poking the soft white flesh
you steal a pinch
watch the colour change
putting your ear to skin
in quiet concentration, listening
for a trace, a murmur, a sign.
You fashion your head
laying down on a different spot
disappointed at the nothing inside me.
You raise your hands to your shoulders
palms upwards
level your long lashes
and shake your two-year-old head
all gone?
And you are wiser than all the adults
seeing more in my silent innards
than they, with their years and education.
Yes, I say, covering my shame, *all gone*.
But you have already forgiven me
plucking your dodi from its dangling chain
you take ... one ... long ... suck
then offer me your comforter
knowing, right now, how much I need it.

Song of the Siamang

I break the red wax seal
take out my mother's ears
wrapped in tissue paper.
Those eighteen-carat-gold earrings
with their inlaid fragment of ruby – still attached.
I press my lips to her left ear – close my eyes
and let the words slip from my tongue
for years they've been growing mould inside me.
I repeat my message into her right ear
a little louder, so she catches every word
as the traffic flows down the Tanyard
the noise of twenty years filtered
to leave just my voice
pressed against her hammer and anvil
long dust within the earth.
I only wish I had kept her lips
so they could tell me that she'd heard.
Or her eyes, so that I could see she understood.
Or perhaps a hand, just one
to curl a finger rhythmically in my hair.
Tonight I'll wear her ears
like earrings dangling from my own
shake my head to feel their movement
caress her lobes and mine
step out under the stillness
of this full moon
my throat sac opening
screaming my words into the earth
and in the morning – listen to their echo.

POETRY LIBRARY

Sold

She gave away her second eldest
to cousins, on in years
with a hotel
a fall of ground to the river
money with no heirs.
He'd be set for life
and they took care of him
that first year when she was so weak
she couldn't lift a cup to her lips
not to mind a hungry baby
to her aching breasts.
It's for the best – the aunts told her
at twelve months – the cousins were all he knew.
It didn't work out that way though.
He went off the rails in his teenage years
accosting his brothers and sisters
calling them Jew bastards, heirs to the throne
left school, lived in a bottle, blamed her
for abandoning him, erasing him.
She tried to explain
the piece of herself that had been
ripped out – where his roots were.
His first curl hidden in the top drawer
not her first born, or her fourth born
or her sixth born, but his
wrapped in tissue paper
touched and prayed over
smelled and cried over
for thirty years
for a hotel
a fall of ground to the river
a few bob.

The Sergeant's Wife

She angled the mirror
taking care not to reflect her lust.
Over cold October nights he was habit-forming
always undressing by the corner chair
draping his braces and trousers over the arm
– prevented creases.
Allowed her marvel at his reflected body
closing her eyes at his glance
then slowly opening
watching his chest muscles tighten
as he bent to remove his underwear
she'd feel the heat crawl beneath the patchwork quilt
brushing against her calves, caressing her inner thighs
spreading up her body.
A sharp intake at the cold rise of the covers
before the heat of him settled inches from her back.
She'd wait his turn, praying his arms
would gather up her nightdress, pull her to him.
Cold and empty those nights he faced the wall
leaving only the rhythm of his breathing
and the strangely soothing feel
of hair on the backs of her legs.

Ecliptic

Our daughter draws crop circles
on the hotel stationery
reminding me that we were married
on December twenty-first
the day the sun stood still
the warmest day
stunning after weeks of rain.
Your father, regal in his
soft cap and matching scarf,
your mother, my maid of honour
a role she had never fulfilled
and you and I after twenty years
saying 'I do' as though
we were new and shiny
looking into each other's eyes
knowing nothing would ever
be the same again.
Afterwards in the hospice
his red rose buttonhole
pinned to his paisley pyjamas
your father told us to go,
waving his handkerchief as though
we were embarking on a voyage,
he sang a verse of
Limerick You're a Lady
his voice unnaturally low
but clear and crisp
like those expanding circles
growing outwards, touching
space beyond the page.

The Last Lie

You were drowning
the quilt like waves
lapping at your nose
I brought you buckets full of air
poured one after another
but the quilt kept rising
you begged me, *please, please*
between gasps, *open the window, please.*
I looked down the ward
between the neat rows of beds
the bodies talking and laughing
the world going on
but you were still drowning
and I couldn't bring myself to rise
open the window
pretend to you or I that this
was going to make the difference.
So I lied, the one thing I could never do.
And when I looked again
the window was open
the waves pouring in
everywhere was water
your face below the surface
your eyes wide – staring up.

Mother's Day in Inchigeela

It was that Mother's Day
when I was too busy
being a mother myself
when, for the first time
you had been the furthest
thing from my thoughts.
All morning I had spent
getting ready for our road trip
the day just stepping forward
as days often do.
On our way, Holly talked to her new
imaginary friend – Nonie
which was strange
because that was another
one of your best friends.
Anna told us about the music box
that woke the house
and played your favourite tune – Für Elise.
She tried but failed to get the box
to play a reminder I didn't need
but just before we left
the box waiting on the kitchen table
burst into life, and we laughed
as Holly and Darby danced.
On the way we stopped by your grave
to say hello. Darby introduced Holly
to his big brother and she laughed and said
I know baby Louie – he's an angel.
We sang to keep the kids entertained
the road to Inchigeela
being so much longer than expected
and just when it seemed endless
Darby saw Louie's torch beam from heaven
and indeed the clouds sported a shaft of light
and every bend seemed to take us closer.

Finally arrived
the children found the farm fascinating
descending like a pack of marauding dogs
I let Anna do the talking, funerals and death
never being within my comfort zone
and there was genuine delight
at seeing us, for making the journey
and I couldn't believe when Anna
told them about the music box
and Louie's torch beam from heaven
and when one of her daughters said
I saw that too and I was thinking of my dad.
And there was tea and Jaffa Cakes
and talks of the old days
when you and Kathleen were friends
when you chose her to be my Godmother
the only one who never forgot.
And Anna remembering Kathleen's wedding
she would have been just five –
because it was October –
and I knew by Kathleen's look
that she didn't believe her
and yet, when they dug out the album
there she was, front row in the group photo
and you wearing your 'Witchy Poo' hat
and smiling out at me
as if all day you were waiting
for that page to open.

Just Listening

She had a man in her attic
where the rafters sloped to their lowest point
in at the corner, crouched.
He talked to her
usually when she least expected it.
He had an accent, Asian origin.
He read fortune cookies
told her when she should sing
when the bees in her garden were idle
when watermelons ripened outside.
She liked having him there
it combated the loneliness
the routine that kept her going –
but threatened to kill her.
He was her sanity.
She liked to take her clothes off
climb her 'Stira' into the air that hinted of him
pull up the ladder, heave the springs closed
to lie on the bare chipboard floor
and listen to him breathe
calm, quiet breaths that sang
of mountains rolling with grass – people-less
where his fingers strummed each blade
filling the air with his harmony.

ChildLine

It was there in the mist
rising off the garden shed
the songs of birds
the sleep swirling from my head
I heard the crackle of the line
as if from a great distance
degraded by the passing years
to just a whisper
mangled by the waking day
the distant traffic
the noise of neighbours' wheelie bins.
I strain to hear, to pick one word
one syllable of sound
one note to register it's you.
As if I could hold the morning
to my ear, squeeze it hard
the tyres on tarmac fading out
the sound of my own breathing
the drip of cistern water
wearing back the folded years
to days, minutes, seconds
and back again to before you spoke
to seconds, minutes, years
before it happened
and winding slowly forward
until before the time could come
you'd make that call
the static all but gone.

The day the grand-aunts came to dinner

my mother raced between the starched tablecloth and
the steam, rinsing the walls in the back kitchen. We were
under starter's orders not to open our mouths so we
stared from the sidelines at the delicate way they lifted
their soup spoons to their lips and silently
drank. There was no noise at all and I became so
conscious of my own breathing and the noise my
throat made when I swallowed spit that I nearly wet
myself with fear that my mother's hand would whip out
and clip me. My father arrived late and scraped
his chair along the floor, rocked the table and my
mother's glare, as he seated himself. *What's this shit?*
he asked, pointing to the soup. My mother smiled, a thin
pained smile to all seated, and continued eating, her grip
and twist of the bread the only outer sign of her distress.
My father slurped, and even though I
was only seven, I knew he was doing it intentionally.
His presence had charged the air and the grand-aunts'
movements seemed more mechanical, arthritic,
almost painful. *So,* he announced, as if everyone
knew what the conversation was. Nobody met his
gaze, well, none of the aunts anyway. My mother
glared from the top of the table and I had the feeling she
wished she was close enough to kick him. Grand-
aunty Jo, with the bright-red lipstick and matching
shoes, was the only one to rest her spoon and take
his stare. *What would you like us to say, Denis?* she
asked, and I realised I had been holding my breath
the whole time and must have been close to blue because
it pained terribly when I let it slip between
my lips, out into the frost of the kitchen. *It wasn't our
place to tell you, really, you can't hold us responsible. To
tell me what,* my father whispered, *that I have a sister?*
And I felt I had missed part of the conversation, I had
fallen asleep and they were talking about someone

else, because not now, after I had always longed for an aunt, could she materialise like a genie from the steam of the soup, a half-century dropped from the heavens.

If I was your daughter

I would wrap my arms around your neck
press my lips to your cheek and squeeze.
I would spend hours playing with your black hair
tying ribbons, plaits, curls
disbelieving stories of your childhood blonde.
I would tell you news in my child's voice
rambling on about the tree house in the lawn
too high even for my long legs.
I would hold your man hand on family days
and you would know my silence spelled contentment.

You would listen, really listen
when I argued out my growing beliefs.
You would know how to love me
you would never tell me
you'd drown my dog while I was at school.
You would always say, *yes*
when I asked for the school-tour money
or explained if you said, *no*.
You wouldn't expect me to fulfil the role of servant
to you or any man.
You would show pride in my smallest achievement
you would know me, my life, my friends
as much as any father can.

And I would know you loved me
without words, without judgement.
I would not judge your old ways
cast a dark eye in disbelief
I would not make you feel small
frightened of my child knowledge
I would not sit and sulk or bull-arse
at a throwaway comment said to amuse
I would not choose sides between you and my mother
judging without the love she possessed for you
I would worship you as my hero
If I was your daughter.

Perfection

I'm here sorting clothes
I haven't seen in nearly nine months.
Then, they were exactly what I wanted to wear
now, they no longer fit my altered self
even though buttons close
they represent a different me
the old, immature, forty-year-old.
Now, a mystery even to myself
my voyage will not happen in these clothes
my favourite Only jeans
cannot express the dance my feet crave
my Savida blouse doesn't reflect
a woman on the edge of laughter.
I am reborn. In need of a 0-45 Babygro
pink, with exposed feet and a soft white collar.
I want a bunny head on my left breast
whose ears are loose and floppy
and fasteners all the way down
to flower covered socks, with padded soles
and frills – did I mention frills? –
rows of them, covering my rear
and then I will pull my legs
into the body of this suit
and sleep the sleep of the dead
in preparation.

Language

This morning, I felt I should
bless myself before breakfast
my customary cornflakes
replaced by the full Irish
and ewes leading their lambs
to ground.
Last night I met a woman
who said she dreamt in Irish
and I felt cheated, deprived
by the Englishman with the
handlebar moustache
crunching toast at the next table.
Deprived of *fadas* in my sleep
of the erotic dreams
I would have had, *as Gaeilge*.
Instead I couldn't dream
my famine-conscious mind
refusing to participate
in the *Sasanach* fantasy
leaving me exhausted
embittered against a generation
who learn of peace talks
Stormont and disarmament
and I realise I'm the old man
at Molly Darcy's
watching the last twenty minutes
of Ireland versus England
shouting about the British bastards
who starved the country
leaving us to rot in potato blight
and absentee landlords.
I am looking for the *poll dubh*
in the universe. The excuse for
my laziness. I am looking for
the *daoine bochta* but all around me
prosper. Not coring out the black
stench of blight to find the sip of
sustenance. *Tá mé ag iarraidh feabhsú.*

I want to dream *as Gaeilge*
I want to know who, at my very core
I am. And as my cholesterol sings
coursing through my body are strings
of data, hard coded in my cells
and I know, at that level
I speak only one language.

fadas: a dash or punctuation mark over a vowel in Irish
as Gaeilge: in Irish
Sasanach: English
poll dubh: black hole
daoine bochta: poor people
Tá mé ag iarraidh feabhsú: I'm trying to improve

No Longer Sexy

I've stopped writing sexy poems
my inspiration has turned to
war, motherhood, wife.
I've forgotten to undress, a staple of myself.
Now I write sensible knicker poems
big and long and covering everything.
There is no fringe of lace
no hint of furtive longing
no whisper of lust between the lines.
I look at fit verse and think
that should be me
but I've lost the art of seduction
I'm naked now, baring all
my imperfections
rippling white pillows of skin
hairy legs and armpits and chins
a stretch-marked zebra
cantering through the Serengeti
flashing my rump at disinterested herbivores
knowing there is no chase in them
yet hoping they'll see something in me
I can't find in myself.

Crossroads – Folklore from Kerry
Real Imaginings – a Kerry anthology, edited by Tommy
Frank O'Connor
Touching Stones – Liam Ryan
Where the Music Comes From – Pat Galvin
No Place Like It – Hugh O'Donnell
The Moon Canoe – Jerome Kiely
Watching Clouds – Gerry Boland
Via Crucis – David Butler
Capering Moons – Anatoly Kudryavitsky
I Shouldn't be Telling You This – Mae Leonard
Notes Towards a Love Song – Aidan Hayes
Meeting Mona Lisa – Tommy Frank O'Connor

Every DOGHOUSE book costs €12, postage free,
to anywhere in the world (& other known planets).
Cheques, Postal Orders (or any legal method) payable
to DOGHOUSE, also PAYPAL (www.paypal.com) to
doghousepaypal@eircom.net

"Buy a full set of DOGHOUSE books, in time they will
be collectors' items" - Gabriel Fitzmaurice, April 12,
2005.

DOGHOUSE
P.O. Box 312
Tralee G.P.O.
Tralee
Co. Kerry
Ireland
tel + 353 6671 37547
email doghouse312@eircom.net
www.doghousebooks.ie